TRAIN YOUR BRAIN LOGIC PUZZLES

Sharpen your logical reasoning skills and have fun with these engaging deduction puzzles.

Great for anyone who loves a good mental challenge!

Perfect for fans of brain teasers, creative thinking, and critical thinking games, each puzzle encourages you to make connections, analyze clues, and think flexibly.

Ideal for classrooms (a great fast finisher activity!), therapy sessions, or independent enrichment, these puzzles support executive function, reasoning, and problem-solving skills.

Puzzles created by three Speech Language Pathologists who specialize in Cognitive Rehabilitation Therapy. Look for the answer key at the end of the book.

Created by:

April Crystal MS, CCC/SLP

Emily Harrison MS, CCC/SLP

Michelle Huish MS, CCC/SLP

Helpful Hints for Completing Logic Puzzles

1. **Use all information:**
   All items and facts listed in the clues will be used somewhere in the puzzle.

2. **Identify pairs:**
   Look for items or facts that need to stay together.

3. **Use the graph:**
   Check the clues and the graph to see where items or facts can fit in the puzzle.

4. **Start easy:**
   Fill in the given items and facts first.

5. **Take breaks:**
   If you feel stuck, step away and come back with fresh eyes and a rested brain.

6. **Read aloud:**
   Sometimes hearing the clues helps you process the details.

7. **Mark used clues:**
   Cross off what you've already solved so you know what's done and what still needs your attention.

8. **Underline/highlight key items:**
   Mark or write down the items you're working with to keep track of possibilities and connections.

9. **Make notes:**
   Write down possibilities or non-possibilities in the graph.

10. **Stay systematic:**
Identify the category with the fewest blanks or unknowns and focus on solving it first—it often unlocks the rest of the puzzle.

11. **Pay attention to names:**
Be careful not to mix up similar names.

12. **Place information carefully:**
Make sure the correct details go in the correct box or category.

13. **Double-check:**
Confirm your solution matches *all* the clues.

Train Your Brain - Level 3 - Book 2 - Logic Puzzle # 1 Clues

1. Peggy's favorite Broadway show is *Chicago*.
2. Eliza does not wear jeans or a chiffon dress to her favorite show.
3. Christine's favorite Broadway song is not "My Shot."
4. Nala's favorite Broadway song is "Music of the Night."
5. The woman whose favorite Broadway show is *Into The Woods* wears jeans when she goes.
6. Eliza's favorite Broadway song is "Defying Gravity."
7. The woman whose favorite Broadway song is "Agony" wears a wool sash to her favorite show.
8. Glinda's favorite Broadway show is *Les Miserables*.
9. Peggy wears a little black dress when she goes to her favorite show.
10. Glinda's favorite Broadway song is "Agony."
11. The woman whose favorite Broadway song is "I Dreamed a Dream" loves the Broadway show *Wicked*.
12. Angelica's favorite Broadway show is *Hamilton*.
13. Christine wears hair bows every time she goes to her favorite show.
14. The woman whose favorite Broadway song is "All That Jazz" wears a chiffon dress to her favorite show.
15. The woman whose favorite Broadway show is *Phantom of the Opera* wears satin pants when she goes to a Broadway show.

Train Your Brain - Level 3 - Book 2 - Logic Puzzle # 1

	Angelica	Eliza	Peggy	Nala	Glinda	Christine
Favorite Broadway Show						
Favorite Thing to Wear to the Show						
Favorite Broadway Song						

Train Your Brain - Level 3 - Book 2 - Logic Puzzle # 2 Clues

1. Eleanor wants to go fishing and will sleep in her green tent.
2. The woman whose favorite camping food is hot dogs is camping in Yosemite.
3. Dorothy likes to eat trail mix.
4. The woman who has an orange tent is not camping in Zion National Park.
5. Mildred wants to go canoeing and her favorite camping food is chili.
6. The woman camping in the Great Smoky Mountains does not like to eat corn on the cob.
7. Helen has a red tent and is camping in Moab.
8. The woman whose favorite camping food is marshmallows wants to go hiking.
9. The woman who has a yellow tent is camping in the Great Smoky Mountains.
10. Ruth wants to go birdwatching in Glacier National Park.
11. The woman who has a blue tent wants to do some stargazing.

Train Your Brain - Level 3 - Book 2 - Logic Puzzle # 2

	Ruth	Eleanor	Helen	Mildred	Dorothy
Camping Location					
Activity					
Favorite Camping Food					
Tent Color					

Train Your Brain - Level 3 - Book 2 - Logic Puzzle # 3 Clues

1. The woman whose name means "joy" does not like the Harvest Festival.
2. Moon's favorite crystal is Amethyst, and her spirit animal is the owl.
3. The woman whose name means "dreams" does not have the wolf as her spirit animal.
4. Meadow's favorite crystal is Moonstone, and her favorite festival is Earth Day.
5. The woman whose spirit animal is a butterfly has a name that means "growth."
6. River's name means "peace," and she loves the Labradorite.
7. The woman who likes the Drum Circle Festival likes Citrine.
8. Sunshine's spirit animal is the fox.
9. Willow's name means "strength," and she loves the Poetry Reading Festival.
10. The woman whose spirit animal is a deer loves Rose Quartz.
11. The woman whose name means "dreams" loves the Winter Solstice Festival.

Train Your Brain - Level 3 - Book 2 - Logic Puzzle # 3

	Willow	Moon	River	Sunshine	Meadow
Meaning of Their Name					
Favorite Crystal					
Spirit Animal					
Favorite Festival					

Train Your Brain - Level 3 - Book 2 - Logic Puzzle # 4 Clues

1. Emmett enjoys taking pictures on rooftops, but he does not use books as props.
2. The man who uses a Nikon camera takes pictures in the forest.
3. Jacob uses umbrellas as props and a telephoto lens.
4. One man uses vintage suitcases as props and a wide-angle lens.
5. Alex uses a Canon camera and a fisheye lens.
6. The man who uses a prime lens does not use a Sony camera.
7. Gabriel uses mirrors as props and takes pictures at abandoned buildings.
8. The man who uses a Canon camera does not take pictures on city streets.
9. Liam uses bicycles as props and a Polaroid camera.
10. Someone takes pictures on the beach.
11. One man uses a macro lens with his Leica camera.

Train Your Brain - Level 3 - Book 2 - Logic Puzzle # 4

	Emmett	Jacob	Liam	Gabriel	Alex
Type of Camera					
Props They Use					
Where They Take Pictures					
Type of Lens					

Train Your Brain - Level 3 - Book 2 - Logic Puzzle # 5 Clues

1. The person who is allergic to peanuts doesn't have pen-clicking or people who talk during movies as pet peeves.
2. Tim is allergic to wheat and can't stand people who cut in line.
3. Kristy collects books and is allergic to shellfish, but not milk.
4. The person who collects coins is allergic to wheat.
5. Shane collects stuffed animals and dislikes when people leave drawers open.
6. The person who is allergic to eggs collects cars and goes crazy when people chew gum loudly.
7. Jack collects knives, can't stand pen-clicking, and is allergic to something other than eggs.
8. The person who has a pet peeve of people leaving lights on, collects toy ducks and is allergic to strawberries.
9. Cam doesn't mind people who chew gum loudly.

Train Your Brain - Level 3 - Book 2 - Logic Puzzle # 5

	Tim	Shane	Beth	Jack	Cam	Kristy
Collections						
Allergy						
Pet Peeve						

Train Your Brain - Level 3 - Book 2 - Logic Puzzle # 6 Clues

1. Amelia's name has German origins.
2. Adam does not like science fiction or western movies.
3. Beau is organized but not patient or elegant.
4. The athletic person likes to watch romance movies.
5. Adam is not from Belgium.
6. The person who likes science fiction movies is from Denmark, not Austria.
7. Beau's name does not have Hebrew origins.
8. Audrey loves action movies but is not patient.
9. Amelia does not like romance or western movies.
10. Audrey's name has English origins, not French.
11. The person who likes western movies is from Finland, not Belgium.

Train Your Brain - Level 3 - Book 2 - Logic Puzzle # 6

	Adam	Amelia	Beau	Audrey
Where They Live				
Origin of Their Name				
Personality Trait				
Favorite Movie Genre				

Train Your Brain - Level 3 - Book 2 - Logic Puzzle # 7 Clues

1. The nurse went to school for 8 years and attended Johns Hopkins.
2. The general practitioner did not have Professor Woodruff.
3. The person who attended UNLV also had Professor Hansen.
4. The general practitioner completed more than 10 years of school and now works in a skilled nursing facility.
5. The person who liked Dr. Alvarez went to school for 8 years, not 12.
6. The radiologist does not work in the Emergency Room.
7. The physician's assistant loved her professor, Dr. Carn, but she did not attend UCLA.
8. Someone attended Penn State.
9. The physician's assistant works in a pediatric office, not an orthopedic hospital.
10. The person who liked Dr. Woodruff went to school for 14 years, not 10 years.

Train Your Brain - Level 3 - Book 2 - Logic Puzzle # 7

	Years of School	Work Location	University	Favorite Professor
General Practitioner				
Nurse				
Radiologist				
Physician's Assistant				

Train Your Brain - Level 3 - Book 2 - Logic Puzzle # 8 Clues

1. Mabel does not ride in North Carolina.
2. Frank owns a Specialized bike, not a Canyon bike.
3. San Diego is where the Belgian Waffle Ride bike trail is located.
4. The Whole Enchilada bike trail is in Moab.
5. Rose rides the A-Line bike trail.
6. The Black Mountain bike trail is not located in Belgium.
7. Someone rides their Ibis bike on The Whole Enchilada bike trail.
8. Mabel rides a Trek bike.
9. The person who rides a Specialized bike rides in New Zealand.
10. Mabel's favorite bike trail is Tour of Flanders.
11. Theo enjoys riding his Yeti bike, but he's never ridden the Old Ghost bike trail.
12. The person who rides a Santa Cruz bike rides in Canada.
13. Julia rides the Belgian Waffle Ride bike trail.

Train Your Brain - Level 3 - Book 2 - Logic Puzzle # 8

	Julia	Frank	Mabel	Rose	Theo	Marilyn
Type of Bike They Own						
Favorite Bike Trail						
Location of Bike Trail Where They Ride						

Train Your Brain - Level 3 - Book 2 - Logic Puzzle # 9 Clues

1. Led Zeppelin's first album was released in 1971, but their drummer's first name is not Dave.
2. The band whose drummer's first name is Alex required M&Ms backstage with all of the brown M&Ms removed.
3. Fleetwood Mac was not the first band to own a private jet, but another band was.
4. The Beatles have the most #1 hits of any band.
5. One of the bands released their first album in 1974.
6. The band whose drummer's first name is John did not have two "classic" eras, but another band did.
7. The band whose drummer's first name is Roger performed at Live Aid.
8. One of the band's first albums was released in 1984, and they required M&Ms backstage with all of the brown M&Ms removed.
9. Fleetwood Mac's first album was released in 1977 and their drummer's name is Mick.
10. The band whose first album was released in 1991 was inducted into the Rock and Roll Hall of Fame in 2014.
11. The band whose drummer's first name is Ringo released their first album in 1967.
12. Queen was the only one of these bands to perform at Live Aid.
13. Nirvana's first album was released in 1991.

Train Your Brain - Level 3 - Book 2 - Logic Puzzle # 9

	Queen	Nirvana	Fleetwood Mac	The Beatles	Led Zeppelin	Van Halen
Year of Their First Album						
Drummer's First Name						
Something Unique About the Band						

Train Your Brain - Level 3 - Book 2 - Logic Puzzle # 10 Clues

1. Someone's favorite candy bar was introduced in Australia and has the tagline "It's the way it shatters."

2. Mae does not like Nestle's Lion chocolate bars.

3. Someone's favorite candy bar was introduced in Japan and it has the tagline "A big hit of cocoa."

4. Mae's favorite candy bar was introduced in 1994, and Sue's was introduced in 1929.

5. Grace's favorite candy bar has the tagline "Have a break."

6. The Kit Kat chocolate bar was introduced in the UK in 1935.

7. Sue's favorite candy bar's tagline is not "Feed the lion."

8. Someone's favorite candy bar is a Black Thunder chocolate bar.

9. Someone's favorite candy bar is Violet Crumble, which was introduced in 1913, not 1935.

10. The Cadbury Crunchie chocolate bar's tagline is "Get that Friday feeling."

11. Ann's favorite candy bar was introduced in 1976.

12. Mae's favorite candy bar was introduced in Japan.

13. Sue, Grace, and Ann's favorite candy bars were introduced in the United Kingdom.

Train Your Brain - Level 3 - Book 2 - Logic Puzzle # 10

	Grace	Mary	Mae	Sue	Ann
Favorite Chocolate Bar					
Year it was Introduced					
Country Where it was Introduced					
Famous Tag Line					

Train Your Brain - Level 3 - Book 2 - Logic Puzzle # 11 Clues

1. The child who likes Super Smash Bros loves their stuffed lizard.
2. Cade and his best friend Luke like their matching stuffed pterodactyls.
3. Gary's best friend is Oliver.
4. Charlotte's best friend is not Sophie.
5. Eva and her best friend like playing The Legend of Zelda.
6. Carter likes his stuffed frog.
7. The child who plays Mario Kart likes his stuffed elephant.
8. Someone likes playing Fortnite.
9. Carter's best friend is Nick.
10. Charlotte likes her stuffed octopus.
11. The child who plays Minecraft likes their stuffed pterodactyl.
12. Monica loves her stuffed butterfly and playing Roblox.
13. Kate's best friend is Grace.
14. Gary likes his stuffed elephant.

Train Your Brain - Level 3 - Book 2 - Logic Puzzle # 11

	Gary	Kate	Charlotte	Carter	Monica	Cade
Best Friend						
Favorite Stuffed Animal						
Favorite Video Game						

Train Your Brain - Level 3 - Book 2 - Logic Puzzle # 12 Clues

1. The man with no siblings wished to explore caves as a child.
2. One of the men who wanted to learn to juggle has only 1 sibling.
3. Oliver is considered an "inventive" man.
4. Someone has 5 siblings, but they do not wear Hoka shoes.
5. Liam, who is "thoughtful," prefers Nike shoes.
6. The man who wished to go to Disneyland as a child is not considered to be "adventurous".
7. Gideon, who wished to learn to juggle as a child, is considered to be "friendly".
8. Arlo prefers Reebok shoes.
9. The man who likes New Balance shoes has 2 siblings.
10. Ethan, who wished to become a magician as a child, is not considered the most "confident" person.
11. The "friendly" man prefers Saucony shoes.
12. Gideon does not have 1 or 3 siblings, but other men do.
13. Mason, who is "curious," prefers Adidas shoes.
14. The man who is "thoughtful" wished for a puppy as a child.
15. Mason and Gideon both had the same childhood wish.
16. Arlo has 4 siblings.

Train Your Brain - Level 3 - Book 2 - Logic Puzzle # 12

	Mason	Ethan	Liam	Arlo	Gideon	Oliver
Personality Trait						
Favorite Shoe						
Childhood Wish						
Number of Siblings						

Train Your Brain - Level 3 - Book 2 - Logic Puzzle # 13

1. The man who loves *Moby Dick* lives in New York.
2. The man who has 1 sibling loves reading *The Great Gatsby.*
3. Mark loves *Huckleberry Finn* and has 6 siblings.
4. The man who has 7 siblings has the last name Dickens and reads *Great Expectations.*
5. Herman's last name is Melville and he has 10 siblings.
6. The man, with the last name Fitzgerald, lives in Minnesota.
7. James' favorite book is Ulysses and he doesn't have Hemingway as a last name.
8. The man who lives in Florida has 5 siblings and loves *The Old Man and the Sea.*
9. The man who has the last name Twain lives in Missouri.
10. F. Scott's last name is Fitzgerald.
11. Charles doesn't live in Missouri.
12. James Joyce lives in Ireland and has 9 siblings.
13. Ernest lives in Florida, unlike someone who lives in England.

Train Your Brain - Level 3 - Book 2 - Logic Puzzle # 13

	Charles	Mark	Ernest	James	F. Scott	Herman
Where They Live						
Favorite Book						
Last Name						
Number of Siblings						

Train Your Brain - Level 3 - Book 2 - Logic Puzzle # 14 Clues

1. It took one person 22 hours to drive to their destination.
2. The person who traveled to San Diego did not listen to "I'm Gonna Be 500 Miles."
3. Esther listened to "Don't Stop Believin'" as she ate grapes, and drove to Georgia.
4. The person who drove 8 hours listened to "On The Road Again" as they traveled.
5. Flora drove 17 hours to her destination.
6. Kendall snacked on carrots while he drove to his destination.
7. The person who drove to Jackson Hole drove three hours less than the person who had the longest drive.
8. The person who snacked on cheese drove to Tennessee, but it did not take them 29 hours to drive there.
9. The person who snacked on raisins listened to "Life is a Highway" while they drove.
10. Sadie's road-trip song was "I'm Gonna Be 500 Miles."
11. The person who drove to Alabama, snacked on Cheezits, and listened to "Send Me On My Way" during their road trip.
12. Someone listened to "Go Your Own Way" while on their road trip.
13. Marge drove 2 hours to Minneapolis.
14. Jenny drove to Jackson Hole and snacked on granola.

Train Your Brain - Level 3 - Book 2 - Logic Puzzle # 14

	Kendall	Marge	Sadie	Flora	Esther	Jenny
Road Trip Destination						
Snacks They Ate						
Hours They Drove						
Travel Song						

Train Your Brain - Level 3 - Book 2 - Logic Puzzle # 15 Clues

1. The woman who reads *Northanger Abbey* does not like brown dresses.
2. Jane loves the novel *Emma*, which was published in 1815.
3. The woman who loves the town of London loves rose-colored dresses.
4. *Northanger Abbey* and *Persuasion* were both published in 1817.
5. Lydia loves the novel *Pride and Prejudice* and the English town of Cambridge.
6. Kitty and Mary like books that were published the same year.
7. Mary does not like *Northanger Abbey*, but she does like the town of Oxford.
8. Elizabeth loves the English town of Bath and a novel that was published in 1811.
9. The woman who reads *Sense and Sensibility* loves lilac-colored dresses.
10. Mary loves champagne-colored dresses.
11. One woman loves a novel that was published in 1813.
12. Kitty loves the English town of York and violet-colored dresses.

Train Your Brain - Level 3 - Book 2 - Logic Puzzle # 15

	Lydia	Jane	Kitty	Mary	Elizabeth
Favorite Dress Color					
Favorite English Town					
Favorite Jane Austen Novel					
Year Their Favorite Book was Published					

Train Your Brain - Level 3 - Book 2 - Logic Puzzles # 16 Clues

1. Zimbabwe is home to Victoria Falls (fun fact), and its language is Shona.
2. The country with two capitals (fun fact), Sucre and La Paz, does not have both English and Maori as official languages, but another country does.
3. Lithuania, which borders Latvia, has the capital Vilnius and a dish called Cepelinai (potato dumplings).
4. In the country that borders Brazil, you may eat Saltenas (a savory pastry) while speaking Spanish.
5. Greenland has a population of 56,000 (fun fact), and its capital is Nuuk.
6. The country with the capital Vilnius has one-third of its land covered in forest (fun fact), and its language is Lithuanian.
7. New Zealand offers Hangi (food cooked in a pit) and its closest neighbor is Australia.
8. Greenland's language is Greenlandic and its closest neighbor is Canada.
9. The country with the capital Harare borders Mozambique.
10. The country that serves Sadza (porridge served with stew) is not crescent shaped.
11. One country has the capital Wellington; its people are called "Kiwis" (fun fact) and its language is not Spanish.
12. The crescent-shaped country (fun fact) has the capital Zagreb and starts with the same letter as "crescent."
13. The country that serves Suaasat (seal broth) has a population of 56,000 people (fun fact).
14. Croatia's neighboring country is Serbia, its language is Croatian, and it is known for Peka (slow-roasted meat and vegetables).

Train Your Brain - Level 3 - Book 2 - Logic Puzzle # 16

	Croatia	Zimbabwe	Lithuania	Greenland	Bolivia	New Zealand
Capital(s)						
Fun Fact						
Language						
Bordering/ Neighboring Country						
Food To Try if You Go There						

Train Your Brain - Level 3 - Book 2 - Logic Puzzle # 17 Clues

1. Jocelyn does not like to make fried rice.
2. Miles and Elliot both love the movie *Shawshank Redemption.*
3. Clara's last name is Benson.
4. The person with the last name Ward loves watching *It's a Wonderful Life*.
5. Gideon plants corn in his garden and loves to make chili.
6. Miles does not grow spinach in his garden.
7. The woman who loves *My Fair Lady* does not plant asparagus in her garden and does not like to cook hamburgers.
8. Clara likes to make pizza.
9. Elliot Mason grows carrots in his garden.
10. Someone has the last name Reed and they like the movie *Gladiator*.
11. The woman whose last name is Price loves to watch *The Sound of Music* while planting sunflowers in her garden.
12. The man who likes to make tacos has the last name Carter.
13. Gideon does not have the last name Ward.
14. Tessa grows raspberries in her garden and loves to make pancakes.

Train Your Brain - Level 3 - Book 2 - Logic Puzzle # 17

	Elliot	Clara	Jocelyn	Miles	Tessa	Gideon
Favorite Movie						
Last Name						
What They Plant in Their Garden						
Favorite Meal						

Train Your Brain - Level 3 - Book 2 - Logic Puzzle # 18 Clues

1. Writ and Vision sells books and has a half-price sale on coloring books.
2. Collective Underground sells handmade items.
3. Liminal does not have a dozen-lilies sale, but another store does.
4. Board of Provo is open between 9 am and 2 pm and sells longboards.
5. The store that is open between 10 am and 5 pm is managed by Dave.
6. Writ and Vision and Liminal both have a manager named Olivia.
7. Foxglove is open between 10 am and 5 pm and sells flowers.
8. Hruska's, managed by Regan, offers a sale on baker's dozen donuts and is open between 7 am and 2 pm.
9. Collective Underground has a buy 1 get 1 (B1G1) sale on silver rings.
10. The store with Converse 20% off is managed by Elizabeth.
11. Writ and Vision is not open between 3 pm and 9 pm.
12. One of the stores sells frames.
13. The store managed by Ben is not open between 12 pm and 8 pm.
14. Liminal, which is open between 12 pm and 4 pm has buy 2 get 1 free (B2G1) off vases.

Train Your Brain - Level 3 - Book 2 - Logic Puzzle # 18 Clues

	Board of Provo	Writ and Vision	Hruska's	Collective Underground	Liminal	Foxglove
Hours						
Manager Name						
Popular Item Sold						
Special Sale						

Train Your Brain - Level 3 - Book 2 - Logic Puzzle # 19 Clues

1. Jared races on the Donut Plains track.
2. Tiffany never chooses Monster Wheels.
3. Ashley races on the Rainbow Road track and chooses Yoshi as her character.
4. One woman chooses Donkey Kong as her character and drives a Tri-Speeder with Slim Wheels.
5. Ashley and Tiffany both drive a Standard Kart.
6. Jared likes Metal Wheels.
7. One person races on the Bowser's Castle track, driving a Badwagon with Roller Wheels.
8. The woman who races on the Mario Circuit track uses Slick Wheels.
9. One of the women who drives a Standard Kart uses Off-Road Wheels.
10. Amy races on a Jet Bike, but she does not choose Toad as her character.
11. The person who loves Princess Peach races on the Koopa Beach track.
12. The man who races on a Flame Rider chooses Mario as his character.
13. One of the women who drives a Standard Kart likes to be Princess Peach.
14. Landon does not race as Luigi.
15. Lydia races as Donkey Kong on the Ghost Valley track.

Train Your Brain - Level 3 - Book 2 - Logic Puzzle # 19

	Ashley	Amy	Lydia	Jared	Tiffany	Landon
Mario Kart Character						
Track						
Vehicle						
Wheels						

Train Your Brain - Level 3 - Book 2 - Logic Puzzle # 20

1. Joey likes playing Scrabble when his mom won't let him play a video game.
2. Someone plays the video game Tetris and reads the book Eragon.
3. Jace cleans the bathroom before playing the board game Settlers of Catan with friends.
4. The person who cleans kitchen counters likes playing Pac-Man and reading *Wonder.*
5. Ellie and Jace both like playing the video game Super Mario Bros.
6. Joey enjoys reading *The Lord of the Rings.*
7. The person who vacuums likes playing the board game Life.
8. The person who likes playing Monopoly is currently reading *Keeper of the Lost Cities.*
9. The girl who likes to play Super Mario Bros loves the book series *Wings of Fire.*
10. Someone enjoys reading *Percy Jackson*.
11. Jacob, who loves the video game Animal Crossing, does not take out the garbage.
12. The person who sweeps the kitchen floor likes the board game Clue.
13. The person who likes playing the video game Minecraft has to take out the garbage.
14. One of the people who likes Super Mario Bros has to sweep the kitchen floor.
15. Max does not mow the lawn.
16. Kate cleans the kitchen counters before playing the board game Sorry.

Train Your Brain - Level 3 - Book 2 - Logic Puzzle # 20

	Joey	Ellie	Jacob	Jace	Kate	Max
Book						
Chore						
Board Game						
Video Game						

Train Your Brain - Level 3 - Book 2 - Logic Puzzle # 21 Clues

1. The person who prefers running eats Greek yogurt but does not exercise at Move Gym or Power House.
2. Laura works out at Lift Club and snacks on hummus.
3. Adam bikes to Better You and snacks on cheese, not protein bars, after his workout.
4. The person who eats eggs as a snack enjoys walking and attends Move Gym.
5. Samantha faithfully attends yoga class at Strong Zone but avoids snacks that require refrigeration.
6. The Power House member enjoys swimming and drinks milk after every workout.
7. The weightlifter snacks on hummus to help build muscle.
8. Charlotte attends Fit Place and is training for her first marathon.
9. Charles does not exercise at Move Gym.

Train Your Brain - Level 3 - Book 2 - Logic Puzzle # 21

	Charlotte	Samantha	Laura	Adam	Evelyn	Charles
Preferred Exercise						
After Exercise Snack						
Gym Membership						

Train Your Brain - Level 3 - Book 2 - Logic Puzzle # 22 Clues

1. Brenda eats pineapple and loves to dance the foxtrot.
2. The woman who vacations in Cancun listens to country music.
3. Esther loves listening to classic rock music.
4. The woman who dances the waltz vacations in California.
5. Maria loves eating mangoes while vacationing in Fiji.
6. The woman who dances the tango also eats kiwi.
7. The woman who ballet dances does not vacation in Spain.
8. Evelyn eats pomegranate and loves listening to alternative rock music.
9. The woman who vacations in California does not like piano music.
10. Amber loves to dance the salsa and vacations in Scotland.
11. The woman who eats bananas loves listening to rhythm and blues.

Train Your Brain - Level 3 - Book 2 - Logic Puzzle # 22

	Maria	Brenda	Esther	Evelyn	Amber
Favorite Vacation Spot					
Favorite Fruit					
Favorite Type of Music					
Favorite Dance Step					

Train Your Brain - Level 3 - Book 2 - Logic Puzzle # 23 Clues

1. Finn owns a fish.
2. Alex took their pet monkey to the vet.
3. Someone owns a cat and drives a Toyota.
4. Roe owns dogs.
5. Minnie and her partner, Al, drive a Mustang.
6. Julia owns guinea pigs.
7. Charlie drives a Volkswagen.
8. Minnie owns horses.
9. Al does not own a cat.
10. Bree enjoys playing with her dogs.
11. Someone owns dogs and drives a Honda.
12. Tyler enjoys traveling in their corvette.
13. Julia and Sean own a Ferrari.
14. Marc's partner is Kari.

Train Your Brain - Level 3 - Book 2 - Logic Puzzle # 23

	Julia	Finn	Minnie	Roe	Tyler	Marc
Type of Car						
Pet						
Partner's Name						

Train Your Brain - Level 3 - Book 2 - Logic Puzzle # 24 Clues

1. Marianne likes Fresca.
2. The person who drinks Diet Pepsi also likes white chocolate macadamia nut cookies.
3. Ellie does not like turkey sandwiches.
4. The person who eats club sandwiches drinks Fresca.
5. The person who drinks Diet Dr. Pepper likes blondies as her favorite cookie.
6. The person who likes turkey sandwiches drinks Mountain Dew.
7. Katie and Ellie like corn chips.
8. Claire likes Takis and oatmeal cookies.
9. Katie does not like chicken sandwiches.
10. The person who likes Takis and oatmeal cookies likes cheese steak sandwiches.
11. The person who likes tuna sandwiches likes sea salt and vinegar chips.
12. Ellie likes blondies and Marianne likes chocolate chunk cookies.
13. Katie prefers brownies while Allison prefers white chocolate macadamia nut cookies.
14. Claire drinks Powerade.
15. Allison likes sea salt and vinegar chips and Marianne likes pita chips.

Train Your Brain - Level 3 - Book 2 - Logic Puzzle # 24

	Marianne	Allison	Ellie	Katie	Claire
Drink					
Sandwich					
Chips					
Cookie					

Train Your Brain - Level 3 - Book 2 - Logic Puzzle # 25 Clues

1. Wells's favorite book is *The Hobbit,* and his middle name is not Lincoln.
2. The man who lives in Elk Ridge has one brother and one sister, and he loves *Harry Potter*.
3. The man whose middle name is Monroe lives in Salem.
4. Rex's middle name is Jackson.
5. Hank's middle name is Foster, and he has two brothers and no sisters.
6. Drew does not live in Salem or Tooele.
7. The man who loves *Unbroken* lives in Tooele.
8. The man who has one brother and two sisters loves reading *Tuesdays with Morrie.*
9. Clark loves *1984* and he has four younger sisters and no brothers.
10. Ty lives in Elk Ridge, while another person lives in Saratoga.
11. The man who has three brothers and one sister has the middle name Adams, and he does not have a favorite book because he never reads.
12. Wells Madison lives in Highland and has the number of brothers and sisters as Hank.
13. The man named after his father, Jackson, lives in American Fork.

Train Your Brain - Level 3 - Book 2 - Logic Puzzle # 25

	Clark	Ty	Rex	Drew	Hank	Wells
Middle Name						
Number of Brothers and Sisters						
Favorite Book						
Where They Live						

Train Your Brain - Level 3 - Book 2 - Logic Puzzle # 26 Clues

1. The woman who lives in Ohio sleeps 7 hours a night.
2. Amanda speaks Spanish and is not a math teacher.
3. Melissa does not sleep 4 or 6 hours a night, but others do.
4. Anna is a nurse and lives in New Jersey.
5. The hairdresser is fluent in Chinese.
6. Anna and Melissa speak the same language.
7. Rob sleeps 8 hours a night.
8. The person who sleeps 5 hours a night is fluent in Japanese.
9. One of the women who speaks Danish sleeps 4 hours a night.
10. The editor lives in Nevada.
11. Melissa speaks Danish and is an editor.
12. Steven is an insurance agent and does not sleep 9 hours a night.
13. Jessica moved to Alabama after finishing her hairdresser certification.
14. The man who speaks German is not a paralegal and does not live in Montana.
15. Rob just moved to Texas.

Train Your Brain - Level 3 - Book 2 - Logic Puzzle # 26

	Anna	Amanda	Jessica	Rob	Melissa	Steven
Job						
State						
Language						
Sleep						

Train Your Brain - Level 3 - Book 2 - Logic Puzzle # 27 Clues

1. John has brown hair and loves to run.
2. Ben plays the drums and has blonde hair.
3. The curious person plays piano and has straight red hair.
4. Any free time that Robin has is spent reading.
5. Ben is not adventurous or creative.
6. The man who plays the tenor saxophone is very serious.
7. Paul is meticulous in every aspect of his life.
8. The woman with short, straight, black hair plays the flute and is very creative.
9. William, who practices his trumpet for 2 hours a day, has the same color hair as John.
10. The adventurous person likes boating.
11. The person with blonde hair loves fishing.
12. The man who plays the guitar is bald and does not like 4-wheeling.
13. One of the people prefers to spend time on woodworking projects.
14. Laura is curious, which makes it hard for her to be dependable because she loses track of time.

Train Your Brain - Level 3 - Book 2 - Logic Puzzle # 27

	John	William	Robin	Paul	Ben	Laura
Hair Color						
Hobby						
Musical Instrument						
Personality						

Train Your Brain - Level 3 - Book 2 - Logic Puzzle # 28 Clues

1. Maddox won the Manza race in his yellow car.
2. Bridgette's team manager, Sam, teases her about driving the same type of car for races and everyday driving.
3. Milo won Le Mans in his orange Audi.
4. Greg won the 24-hour Nürburgring race and then had his manager, Ty, drive him home in his non-racing car, a Toyota.
5. The woman who drives a red Honda won the Indy 500.
6. Kyle enjoys driving around town in his Bentley with his manager, Jeff.
7. Milo dreams of racing in Monte Carlo, but his manager, Parker, hasn't been able to help make it happen.
8. The person who races in a Ferrari doesn't get along with the team manager, Jake.
9. The person who drives a Volkswagen every day does not have a green race car.
10. The woman who drives a white Hyundai did not win the Daytona race, but she did win a different race.
11. One man drives a blue Chevrolet.
12. The Porsche owner's name and car color start with the same letter.
13. After winning Monte Carlo, the driver left the race with team manager Dave in their everyday car, a Mercedes-Benz.
14. The person who drives a Rolls Royce on a regular basis races in an orange car.

Train Your Brain - Level 3 - Book 2 - Logic Puzzle # 28

	Greg	Maddox	Milo	Bridgette	Maylee	Kyle
Race Car						
Color of Race Car						
Race						
Everyday Car						
Team Manager						

Train Your Brain - Level 3 - Book 2 - Logic Puzzle # 29 Clues

1. George does not like to eat mushrooms.
2. Lisa's childhood best friend is not Allison.
3. Emma loves tacos but hates spaghetti.
4. One woman gets sushi every week with her mom, Julie, and her best friend, Sarah.
5. Emma and Lisa have moms with the same name.
6. Growing up, George's best friend was Henry.
7. The person whose childhood friend is Heidi loves to eat kimchi with his mom, Anne, but does not like rice.
8. The woman who hates eggs has been best friends with Helen since age 11.
9. One of the women whose mom is named Nancy grew up with a best friend named Michelle.
10. Emily's mom is Andrea.
11. The person who loves noodles hates bread.
12. The man whose mom is named Peggy loves to eat pizza but never with mushrooms on it.
13. Lisa, whose mom's name is Nancy, eats noodles every day.
14. Bob does not count salmon as his favorite food, but someone else does.
15. Kali loves sushi but hates stir fry.

Train Your Brain - Level 3 - Book 2 - Logic Puzzle # 29

	Emma	Emily	Kali	George	Lisa	Bob
Favorite Food						
Least Favorite Food						
Mom's Name						
Childhood Best Friend						

Train Your Brain - Level 3 - Book 2 - Logic Puzzle # 30 Clues

1. The person who is a university professor likes water aerobics.
2. Clay's commute time is 37 minutes shorter than the other man's.
3. The person with a poodle has a 45-minute commute to work.
4. The man who mountain bikes goes on 3-hour rides.
5. Summer loves doing yoga with her cat.
6. Brooke, who works as a university professor, has a commute 41 minutes longer than Jared's.
7. Jared does not like snakes, fish, or poodles.
8. The man who owns a goldfish has a 12-minute commute to work as a janitor.
9. The poodle, who lives with a chef, exercises with its owner for 30 minutes a day.
10. Summer does not exercise for 75 minutes.
11. Erika takes her golden retriever, not border collie, on 45-minute hikes.
12. Danielle takes 20 more minutes to get to work than Natalie, who takes 30 minutes less than Erika.
13. The man who does HIIT workouts considered doing a 25-minute workout, but decided to do a 40-minute workout next to his goldfish.
14. Summer's commute to the neighboring school is 10 minutes shorter than Clay's; she works as a teacher's aide.
15. Natalie, who has a turtle, works as a mechanic and then runs for one hour after work each day.
16. Erika, who is a movie director, not an engineer, does not like walking.

Train Your Brain - Level 3 - Book 2 - Logic Puzzle # 30

	Natalie	Danielle	Erika	Clay	Jared	Brooke	Summer
Type of Exercise							
Pet							
Exercise (Amount Of Time)							
Commute Time							
Job							

Train Your Brain - Level 3 - Book 2 - Logic Puzzle # 31 Clues

1. The car with the least horsepower (hp) has 112 hp.
2. The Toyota AW11 MR2 and Mercedes AMG1 have the same engine placement.
3. Jake's car is not mid-engine placement, but two other cars are.
4. Zeke's car was built in Germany and is the newest of the cars.
5. Jake's car has 247 hp.
6. Zeke and Brian's cars have the same engine placement as Jake's car.
7. Josh's car is from the same country as Zeke and Jake's cars.
8. One of the cars is a Porsche 944 Turbo S.
9. Hale's car has the least horsepower.
10. The 2025 car has 621 hp, not 1049 hp like another car.
11. One car was made in Japan.
12. Jake and Hale's cars were built in the 1980s, with Hale's being four years older than Jake's.
13. One car is a 1969 C3 Corvette.
14. Brian's car is the only one made in the USA.
15. The 2025 Audi RS7 has a front-mounted engine, along with two other cars.
16. Josh's car doesn't have 350 hp.
17. Brian drives the oldest car.
18. Josh's Mercedes AMG1 is three years older than Zeke's car.
19. One car was built in 1988 and another in 1984.

Train Your Brain - Level 3 - Book 2 - Logic Puzzle # 31

	Car	Engine Placement	Country of Origin	Year	Horse-power
Zeke					
Jake					
Brian					
Hale					
Josh					

TRAIN YOUR BRAIN LOGIC PUZZLES

ANSWER KEY

Train Your Brain - Level 3 - Book 2 - Logic Puzzle # 1

	Angelica	Eliza	Peggy	Nala	Glinda	Christine
Favorite Broadway Show	Hamilton	Phantom Of The Opera	Chicago	Into The Woods	Les Miserables	Wicked
Favorite Thing To Wear To The Show	Chiffon Dress	Satin Pants	Little Black Dress	Jeans	Wool Sash	Hair Bows
Favorite Broadway Song	All That Jazz	Defying Gravity	My Shot	Music Of The Night	Agony	I Dreamed A Dream

Train Your Brain - Level 3 - Book 2 - Logic Puzzle # 2

	Ruth	Eleanor	Helen	Mildred	Dorothy
Camping Location	Glacier National Park	Yosemite	Moab	Great Smoky Mountains	Zion National Park
Activity	Birdwatching	Fishing	Hiking	Canoeing	Stargazing
Favorite Camping Food	Corn on the Cob	Hot Dogs	Marshmallows	Chili	Trail Mix
Tent Color	Orange	Green	Red	Yellow	Blue

Train Your Brain - Level 3 - Book 2 - Logic Puzzle # 3

	Willow	Moon	River	Sunshine	Meadow
Meaning Of Their Name	Strength	Dreams	Peace	Joy	Growth
Favorite Crystal	Rose Quartz	Amethyst	Labradrite	Citrine	Moonstone
Spirit Animal	Deer	Owl	Wolf	Fox	Butterfly
Favorite Festival	Poetry Reading	Winter Solstice	Harvest	Drum Circle	Earth Day

Train Your Brain - Level 3 - Book 2- Logic Puzzle # 4

	Emmett	Jacob	Liam	Gabriel	Alex
Type Of Camera	Sony	Nikon	Polaroid	Lecia	Canon
Type Of Film	Vintage Suitcase	Umbrella	Bicycle	Mirror	Book
What They Photograph	Rooftop	Forest	City Street	Buildings	Beach
Type Of Lighting	Wide-Angle Lens	Telephoto Lens	Prime Lens	Macro Lens	Fisheye Lens

Train Your Brain - Level 3 - Book 2 - Logic Puzzle # 5

	Tim	Shane	Beth	Jack	Cam	Kristy
Collections	Coins	Stuffed Animals	Cars	Knives	Toy Ducks	Books
Allergy	Wheat	Peanuts	Eggs	Milk	Strawberries	Shellfish
Pet Peeve	People Who Cut In Line	Leave Drawers Open	Loud Gum Chewing	Pen-Clicking	Leave Lights On	People Who Talk During Movies

Train Your Brain - Level 3 - Book 2 - Logic Puzzle # 6

	Adam	Amelia	Beau	Audrey
Where They Live	Austria	Denmark	Finland	Belgium
Origin Of Their Name	Hebrew	German	French	English
Personality Trait	Athletic	Patient	Organized	Elegant
Favorite Movie Genre	Romance	Science Fiction	Westerns	Action

Train Your Brain - Level 3 - Book 2 - Logic Puzzle # 7

	Years Of School	Work Location	University	Favorite Professor
General Practitioner	12	Skilled Nursing Facility	UNLV	Dr. Hansen
Nurse	8	Hospital ER	Johns Hopkins	Dr. Alvarez
Radiologist	14	Orthopedic Hospital	UCLA	Dr. Woodruff
Physician's Assistant	10	Pediatric Office	Penn State	Dr. Carn

Train Your Brain - Level 3 - Book 2 - Logic Puzzle # 8

	Julia	Frank	Mabel	Rose	Theo	Marilyn
Type Of Bike They Own	Canyon	Specialized	Trek	Santa Cruz	Yeti	Ibis
Favorite Bike Trail	Belgian Waffle Ride	Old Ghost	Tour of Flanders	A-Line	Black Mountain	The Whole Enchilada
Location Of Bike Trail Where They Ride	San Diego	New Zealand	Belgium	Canada	North Carolina	Moab

Train Your Brain - Level 3 - Book 2 - Logic Puzzle # 9

	Queen	Nirvana	Fleetwood Mac	The Beatles	Led Zeppelin	Van Halen
Year Of First Album	1974	1991	1977	1967	1971	1984
Drummer's First Name	Roger	Dave	Mick	Ringo	John	Alex
Something About The Band	Only Band To Perform At Live Aid	Inducted Into Rock And Roll Hall Of Fame In 2014	They Had Two "Classic" Eras	Most # 1 Hits By Any Band	First Band To Own Their Own Private Jet	Required M&Ms Backstage With Brown M&Ms Removed

Train Your Brain - Level 3 - Book 2 - Logic Puzzle # 10

	Grace	Mary	Mae	Sue	Ann
Chocolate Bar	Kit Kat	Violet Crumble	Black Thunder	Cadbury Crunchie	Nestle's Lion
Year it was Introduced	1935	1913	1994	1929	1976
Country Where it was Introduced	UK	Australia	Japan	UK	UK
Famous Ad	Have A Break	It's the Way it Shatters	A Big Hit of Cocoa	Get That Friday Feeling	Feed the Lion

Train Your Brain - Level 3 - Book 2 - Logic Puzzle # 11

	Gary	Kate	Charlotte	Carter	Monica	Cade
Best Friend	Oliver	Grace	Eva	Nick	Sophie	Luke
Favorite Stuffed Animal	Elephant	Lizard	Octopus	Frog	Butterfly	Pterodactyl
Favorite Video Game	Mario Kart	Super Smash Bros	The Legend of Zelda	Fortnite	Roblox	Minecraft

Train Your Brain - Level 3 - Book 2 - Logic Puzzle # 12

	Mason	Ethan	Liam	Arlo	Gideon	Oliver
Personality Trait	Curious	Adventurous	Thoughtful	Confident	Friendly	Inventive
Favorite Shoe	Adidas	New Balance	Nike	Reebok	Saucony	Hoka
Childhood Wish	Juggle	Magician	Puppy	Disneyland	Juggle	Explore Caves
Number of Siblings	1	2	3	4	5	0

Train Your Brain - Level 3 - Book 2 - Logic Puzzle # 13

	Charles	Mark	Ernest	James	F. Scott	Herman
Where They Live	England	Missouri	Florida	Ireland	Minnesota	New York
Favorite Book	*Great Expectations*	*Adventures of Huckleberry Finn*	*The Old Man and the Sea*	*Ulysses*	*The Great Gatsby*	*Moby Dick*
Last Name	Dickens	Twain	Hemingway	Joyce	Fitzgerald	Melville
Siblings	7	6	5	9	1	10

Train Your Brain - Level 3 - Book 2 - Logic Puzzle # 14

	Kendall	Marge	Sadie	Flora	Esther	Jenny
Road Trip Destination	San Diego	Minneapolis	Tennessee	Alabama	Georgia	Jackson Hole
Snacks They Ate	Carrots	Raisins	Cheese	Cheezits	Grapes	Granola
Hours They Drove	8 Hours	2 Hours	22 Hours	17 Hours	29 Hours	26 Hours
Favorite Travel Song	On the Road Again	Life is a Highway	I'm Gonna Be 500 Miles	Send Me On My Way	Don't Stop Believing	Go Your Own Way

Train Your Brain - Level 3 - Book 2 - Logic Puzzle # 15

	Lydia	Jane	Kitty	Mary	Elizabeth
Favorite Dress Color	Brown	Rose	Violet	Champagne	Lilac
Favorite English Town	Cambridge	London	York	Oxford	Bath
Favorite Jane Austen Novel	Pride And Prejudice	Emma	Northanger Abbey	Persuasion	Sense And Sensibility
Year Their Favorite Book Was Published	1813	1815	1817	1817	1811

Train Your Brain - Level 3 - Book 2 - Logic Puzzle # 16

	Croatia	Zimbabwe	Lithuania	Greenland	Bolivia	New Zealand
Capital	Zagreb	Harare	Vilnius	Nuuk	Sucre And La Paz	Wellington
Fun Fact	Crescent Shaped	Victoria Falls	⅓ Of Country Is Forest	Just Over 56,000 People	2 Capitals	People Known As "Kiwis"
Language	Croatian	Shona	Lithuanian	Greenlandic	Spanish	English And Maori
Neighbor Country	Serbia	Mozambique	Latvia	Canada	Brazil	Australia
Food To Try If You Go There	Peka (Slow Roasted Meat And Veggies)	Sadza (Porridge) Served With Stew	Cepelinai (Potato Dumplings)	Suaasat (Seal Broth)	Saltenas (Savory Pastry)	Hangi (Food Cooked In A Pit)

Train Your Brain - Level 3 - Book 2 - Logic Puzzle # 17

	Elliot	Clara	Jocelyn	Miles	Tessa	Gideon
Favorite Movie	Shawshank	My Fair Lady	The Sound of	Shawshank	It's A Wonderful	Gladiator

	Redemption		Music	Redemption	Life	
Last Name	Mason	Benson	Price	Carter	Ward	Reed
Garden	Carrots	Spinach	Sunflowers	Asparagus	Raspberries	Corn
Favorite Meal	Fried Rice	Pizza	Hamburgers	Tacos	Pancakes	Chili

Train Your Brain - Level 3 - Book 2 - Logic Puzzle # 18

	Board of Provo	Writ and Vision	Hruska's	Collective Underground	Liminal	Foxglove
Hours	9 - 2	12-8	7 - 2	3 - 9	12 - 4	10 - 5
Manager Name	Elizabeth	Olivia	Regan	Ben	Olivia	Dave
Popular Item Soldl	Longboards	Books	Donuts	Handmade items	Frames	Flowers
Special Sale	Converse 20 % off	Half Off Coloring Books	Bakers Dozen	B1G1 silver rings	B2G1 Vases	Dozen Lilies

Train Your Brain - Level 3 - Book 2 - Logic Puzzle # 19

	Ashley	Amy	Lydia	Jared	Tiffany	Landon
Mario Kart Character	Yoshi	Luigi	Donkey Kong	Mario	Princess Peach	Toad
Track	Rainbow Road	Mario Circuit	Ghost Valley	Donut Plains	Koopa Beach	Bowser's Castle
Vehicle	Standard Kart	Jet Bike	Tri-Speeder	Flame Rider	Standard Kart	Badwagon
Wheels	Monster Wheels	Slick Wheels	Slim Wheels	Metal Wheels	Off-Road Wheels	Roller Wheels

Train Your Brain - Level 3 - Book 2 - Logic Puzzle # 20

	Joey	Ellie	Jacob	Jace	Kate	Max
Book	Lord Of The Rings	Wings Of Fire	Keeper Of The Lost Cities	Percy Jackson	Wonder	Eragon
Chore	Take Out Garbage	Sweep Kitchen Floor	Mow Lawn	Clean Bathroom	Clean Kitchen Counters	Vacuum
Board Game	Scrabble	Clue	Monopoly	Settlers Of Catan	Sorry	Life
Video Game	Minecraft	Super Mario Bros	Animal Crossing	Super Mario Bros	Pac-Man	Tetris

Train Your Brain - Level 3 - Book 2 - Logic Puzzle # 21

	Charlotte	Samantha	Laura	Adam	Evelyn	Charles
Preferred Exercise	Running	Yoga	Weights	Bikes	Walking	Swimming
After Exercise Snack	Greek Yogurt	Protein Bars	Hummus	Cheese	Eggs	Milk
Gym Membership	Fit Place	Strong Zone	Lift Club	Better You	Move Gym	Power House

Train Your Brain - Level 3 - Book 2 - Logic Puzzle # 22

	Maria	Brenda	Esther	Evelyn	Amber
Favorite Vacation Spot	Fiji	Cancun	Spain	California	Scotland
Favorite Fruit	Mango	Pineapple	Kiwi	Pomegranite	Banana
Favorite Type Of Music	Piano	Country	Classic Rock	Alternative Rock	Rhythm And Blues
Favorite Dance Step	Ballet	Foxtrot	Tango	Waltz	Salsa

Train Your Brain - Level 3 - Book 2 - Logic Puzzles # 23

	Julia	Finn	Minnie	Roe	Tyler	Marc
Type Of Car	Ferrari	Volkswagen	Mustang	Honda	Corvette	Toyota
Pet	Guinea Pig	Fish	Horses	Dogs	Monkey	Cats
Partner	Sean	Charlie	Al	Bree	Alex	Kari

Train Your Brain - Level 3 - Book 2 - Logic Puzzle # 24

	Marianne-	Allison	Ellie	Katie	Claire
Drink	Fresca	Diet Pepsi	Diet Dr Pepper	Mountain Dew	Powerade
Sandwich	Club	Tuna	Chicken	Turkey	Cheese Steak
Chips	Pita Chips	Sea Salt Vinegar	Corn Chip	Corn Chips	Takis
Cookie	Chocolate Chunk	White Chocolate Macadamia	Blondies	Brownies	Oatmeal

Train Your Brain - Level 3 - Book 2 - Logic Puzzle # 25

	Clark	Ty	Rex	Drew	Hank	Wells
Middle Name	Monroe	Lincoln	Jackson	Adams	Foster	Madison
Number of Brothers and sisters	4 sisters 0 brothers	1 Brother 1 Sister	1 Brother 2 Sisters	3 Brothers, 1 Sister	2 Brothers 0 sisters	2 Brothers 0 sisters
Favorite Book	*1984*	*Harry Potter*	*Tuesdays With Morrie*	*None*	*Unbroken*	*The Hobbit*
Where They Live	Salem	Elk Ridge	American Fork	Saratoga	Tooele	Highland

Train Your Brain - Level 3 - Book 2 - Logic Puzzle #26

	Anna	Amanda	Jessica	Rob	Melissa	Steven
Job	Nurse	Paralegal	Hair Dresser	Math Teacher	Editor	Insurance Agent
State	New Jersey	Ohio	Alabama	Texas	Nevada	Montana
Language	Danish	Spanish	Chinese	German	Danish	Japanese
Sleep	4 Hours	7 Hours	6 Hours	8 Hours	9 Hours	5 Hours

Train Your Brain - Level 3 - Book 2 - Logic Puzzle # 27

	John	William	Robin	Paul	Ben	Laura
Hair Color	Brown	Brown	Black	Bald	Blonde	Red
Hobby	Running	Boating	Reading	Woodworking	Fishing	4-Wheeling
Musical Instrument	Saxophone	Trumpet	Flute	Guitar	Drum	Piano
Personality	Serious	Adventurous	Creative	Meticulous	Dependable	Curious

Train Your Brain - Level 3 - Book 2 - Logic Puzzle # 28

	Greg	Maddox	Milo	Bridgette	Maylee	Kyle
Race Car	Porsche	Ferrari	Audi	Honda	Hyundai	Chevrolet
Color Of Race Car	Green	Yellow	Orange	Red	White	Blue
Race	24-Hour Nürburgring	Manza	Le Mans	Indy 500	Monte Carlo	Daytona
Everyday Car	Toyota	VW	Rolls Royce	Honda	Mercedes	Bentley
Team Manager	Ty	Jake	Parker	Sam	Dave	Jeff

Train Your Brain - Level 3 - Book 2 - Logic Puzzle # 29

	Emma	Emily	Kali	George	Lisa	Bob
Favorite Food	Tacos	Salmon	Sushi	Pizza	Noodles	Kimchi
Least Favorite Food	Spaghetti	Eggs	Stir Fry	Mushrooms	Bread	Rice
Mom's Name	Nancy	Andrea	Julie	Peggy	Nancy	Anne
Childhood Best Friend	Allison	Helen	Sarah	Henry	Michelle	Heidi

Train Your Brain - Level 3 - Book 2 - Logic Puzzles # 30

	Natalie	Danielle	Erika	Clay	Jared	Brooke	Summer
Exercise (Type)	Running	Walking	Hiking	Hiit Workouts	Mountain Biking	Water Aerobics	Yoga
Pet	Turtle	Poodle	Golden Retriever	Goldfish	Border Collie	Snake	Cat
Exercise (Amount Of Time)	1 Hour	30 Minutes	45 Minutes	40 Minutes	3 Hours	75 Minutes	25 Minutes
Commute Time	25 Minutes	45 Minutes	55 Minutes	12 Minutes	49 Minutes	90 Minutes	2 Minutes
Job	Mechanic	Chef	Movie Director	Janitor	Engineer	University Professor	Teacher's Aide

Train Your Brain - Level 3 - Book 2 - Logic Puzzles # 31

	Car	Engine Placement	Country of Origin	Year	Horsepower
Zeke	Audi	Front	Germany	2025	621
Jake	Porsche	Front	Germany	1988	247
Brian	Corvette	Front	USA	1969	350
Hale	Toyota	Mid	Japan	1984	112
Josh	Mercedes	Mid	Germany	2022	1049

Made in United States
Cleveland, OH
04 November 2026

47647258R00043